An American Entrepreneur

Mr. Joyce Clyde Hall

Founder of Hallmark Cards, Inc.

By Margaret Benedict

authorHOUSE®

AuthorHouse™
1663 Liberty Drive, Suite 200
Bloomington, IN 47403
www.authorhouse.com
Phone: 1-800-839-8640

First published by AuthorHouse 9/22/2008

ISBN: 978-1-4389-0572-3 (sc)

Library of Congress Control Number: 2008907847

Printed in the United States of America
Bloomington, Indiana

This book is printed on acid-free paper.

Cards and photographs courtesy of the Hallmark Archives; Hallmark Cards, Inc.

Dedicated to my husband, Jinx Drda,
and the wonderful family we share:

Ben, Lisa, Chloe, Lilly Benedict—Wil, Elizabeth, Alex, Noah Benedict
Chance, Jenny, Jake, Joy Black—Amos, Molly, Maxine Curlee
Lin, Sandy, Steve Drda—David, Carrie Edwards,
Bill, Jere, Dru, Del, Leistritz—Andy, Kate Parker

My sister: Vivian Canada.

In loving memory of John and Hazel Hausman and Ron Hausman.

Acknowledgments

To Mr. Joyce Clyde Hall who lived a life of such true entrepreneurship so that students might learn from his life and experiences. I'm grateful for the company he started, Hallmark Cards, Inc., and the pictures from their archives that they were willing to share. To Mr. Donald Hall, Sr., Chairman, who fulfilled his father's dream of creating a meeting place called Crown Center. To Mr. J. C. Hall's grandsons, Donald J. Hall, Jr., President and CEO; and Mr. David E. Hall, President of Hallmark's personal expression group, who oversees the wholesale business, and whose leadership continues to encompass the Hallmark tradition of giving the very best.

A most grateful thank you to Kristi Ernsting, Publicity Manager, Hallmark Cards, Inc., who read, coached, and was there to answer any questions I had about the company, so that I might maintain complete integrity with any information I wrote.

For their support with my marketing ideas, I am grateful to Gary and Dale Kirlin, whose Hallmark Gold Crown® stores have graced the shopping centers in the St. Louis area and elsewhere. Your family exemplifies the spirit of entrepreneurship.

Many educators were willing to read my manuscript and gave me constructive feedback. I am indebted for your gift of time: Ercel Cody, Diane Kassel, Rose Ann Weeks, and Beth Feger.

Thank you Dr. Mary Suiter, Manager of Economic Education at the St. Louis Federal Reserve Bank, for giving guidance to my many years of teaching economics to the children in my classroom.

A very special thank you is owed to Gayle A. Voyles, director at the University of Missouri-Kansas City, Center for Economic Education, for her willingness to read my manuscript. I look forward to working with you.

To Joseph A. Peri, Executive Vice President, and Chief Operating Officer of the National Council on Economic Education, for granting permission to state the Standards and Benchmarks in the teacher's guide.

To Kathy Conley, without whose computer expertise I would still be trying to figure out how to create the final copy. Thank you for your many hours of help.

To my best friend from high school, Judy Giles Lane, for her words of encouragement and holding me to the task of writing this book. Continue writing your poems for children.

Special thanks are owed to Jere Leistritz, my sister-in-law, who read the manuscript more than once, and for her professional guidance throughout the entire project. I could not have chosen a more gifted middle school teacher.

Contents

Prologue

Dear Readers,

I know that you have read many biographies since you started school, but my wish is that you will see this book differently. One of the goals of this story is to teach you about the life of a very remarkable man, Joyce Clyde Hall. (I will refer to him in this book as J. C. during his early years, and then out of respect to his later years, I will call him Mr. Hall.)

Perhaps you will recognize his name when I ask if you've ever received or sent a greeting card with the name Hallmark on the back of it. Possibly, you've watched the Hallmark Channel on television, or seen a production of the "Hallmark Hall of Fame." Are you getting a better idea of whom this great individual is?

I have a second goal that struck me as I researched Mr. Hall's life; one that seemed a natural process to teach my readers about a social studies area called economics. One might compare this approach with the construction of a tapestry. I will take the strands of Mr. Hall's life and weave them with the strands of economics as they apply to his life experiences. Therefore, you will find some of the vocabulary in this story that will reference economics. I will print those words in **bold** and give the definitions in italics. An example of this follows. **Economics** *is the study of how people use their scarce resources to satisfy wants. This includes decisions about production, consumption, and distribution of goods and services.*

Are you thinking that economics is of no concern to you? It's important that you realize that it's a subject that will affect you for the rest of your life.

You have already decided how to use your money. For instance, you may have asked yourself if you really want to buy a certain item. Should you save your money or spend it? Is an item offered at a good price? That's economics! Mr. Hall had many lessons in economics to learn as he built Hallmark Cards, Inc.—many good, some costly.

Men and women running for the presidency make most of their speeches about economics—issues like rising taxes, social security, and balancing the budget. Does that sound familiar?

I'm writing this story in the third person, narrative style. However, there will be times when I will step out of that style. I will talk to you about what I have written, or I'll give you something to think about. It will be as though we were having a question-and-answer session together. Those discussion comments will be written in italics.

Thank you for taking the time to read this prologue. I hope it will assist you to understand my goals, or even give you some ideas as you fulfill writing assignments required in your classroom.

Sincerely,
M. Benedict

Chapter 1

Lessons From Poverty

The last words of wisdom his father gave to him before he deserted his family were, "The Lord will provide." J. C. was seven years old. He never really knew why his father left. It was the beginning of Joyce Clyde Hall's lessons from poverty. The first lesson that he learned was that hunger was real when there was little money to buy food. Perhaps the Lord would appreciate a little help called—work. Poverty taught him that immediate gratification wasn't possible. The money he earned was more important to save than to spend. That habit would later prepare him when a business opportunity presented itself. Perhaps his most important lessons were that poverty was an enormous motivator to get him to work, and the sting of being poor could be lessened a bit when you shared it with a loving family. J. C. sometimes observed that when food was scarce, his mother didn't seem very hungry.

He was the middle child of five. One child died in infancy; Rollie was nine years older than J. C.; Bill was seven years older, and Marie was four years younger. Rollie would sometimes bring his younger siblings a special treat from the store where he worked. He became a father to the family.

Joyce Clyde Hall was born on August 29, 1891, in David City, Nebraska, sixty miles west of Omaha. Being named Joyce was not easy for a young man. He was named after a traveling bishop who had come to town about the time of his birth.

J. C. was raised in a house where the only heat was a coal-burning pot-bellied stove. The unheated bedroom where he slept got very cold during the night. It wasn't wise to dress slowly on those cold Nebraska mornings. J. C. would get so cold that he often forgot that summer would make its way to Nebraska again! Outdoor toilets were not easy, either—it made one move quickly!

Summers became a welcoming weather change under those circumstances. There was more food from the garden. Added to the menu would be raspberries and rhubarb, as well as cherries, and plums from their trees. An occasional catfish might be caught in a nearby stream.

His father's parents were good to him. Grandfather Hall would often give him a penny. A penny back then would buy much more than it would today. J. C. remembered well that his grandfather had a strict habit of eating an apple every day at 8:00 p.m. before going to bed. Grandmother Hall sometimes offered J. C. her famous graham bread as a snack on his way home from school. His mother's parents, who lived in Kentucky, came for an occasional visit.

His mother had been raised in Hannibal, Missouri—her maiden name was Nancy Houston, and she was the great niece of Samuel Houston (1793–1863), a soldier and statesman born in Lexington, Virginia.

Nancy had been a teacher before marrying J. C.'s father, George Hall, who had run a hardware store in the small town of Brainard, Nebraska. Business was not good, so the family moved to David City. George Hall was also an itinerant preacher—that means he traveled from place to place. It seemed to J. C. that his father always had money for himself but gave little to the family. That led J. C. to believe that they were poor because his father let them be that way.

If you had gone to school with J. C., you would have found it very different than school today. There were no indoor restrooms. When thirsty, students would simply dip the drinking pitcher in the water bucket, take a drink, and then return the rest to the bucket! The next person would do the same. It was called "shared drinking." There was no homework—which would be the part children today would have enjoyed the most. There certainly were no states or federal tests to worry about. The grading scale was one hundred for perfect and sixty was passing. J. C.'s best grades were in history and geography.

J. C. Hall didn't complete high school, because it was necessary for him to help support the family. The schooling through poverty, however, led him to become one of the most successful entrepreneurs in America. *(An **entrepreneur** is one who risks time, efforts, and funds to bring a product to market).* For J. C., being an entrepreneur meant putting service and quality above making a lot of money. Even as a young man, he treated every business with care. He gave his very best.

When J. C. was eight years old, his first job was as a maid and cook on a farm. The lady was going to have a baby and was not in the best of health. Her husband needed someone to care for her while he worked on the farm. Since it was a dry summer and little food grew in the garden, the meals consisted of green beans and bacon. *(Dear Readers, Just think about it—he would have been in the third grade and was working as a maid and a cook. Do you know someone who is eight, or remember when you were that age? Did you cook or clean house? Have you ever had a job outside your home to help your family buy food?)*

He had a common business that children often have today—selling lemonade. When the circus came to town on Sundays, he sold his lemonade to the audiences. His recipe for making a whole tub of lemonade consisted of the juice of one lemon, a lot of citric acid, and twenty-five cents worth of sugar.

His second job when he was nine years old (about the fourth grade) was working as a salesman for the California Perfume Company—later called Avon. He borrowed five dollars from his grandfather to get into the business. He sold door to door after school. Perfume was not his only product. He sold lemon extract, lilac cologne, soap, and tooth powder. Tooth powder instead of tooth paste was often used at that time for cleaning the teeth.

His economic lesson during that business venture was what "credit risk" meant. **(Credit** *is the ability to buy goods and services and pay for them later.)* Sometimes the ladies would ask him to leave the products, and they would pay him later. They never did. "Cash only" became his only business deal! He turned all of his earnings over to his mother, who at that time was an invalid and in poor health.

Joyce, Marie, and Rollie in front of the Norfolk Store

It wasn't until 1902 that the Hall family left extreme poverty, when they moved to Norfolk, Nebraska. J. C.'s older brothers, Rollie and Bill, had formed a partnership with a man named W. S. Jay. *(A **partnership** is when two or more people operate a business.)* The three men bought a bookstore. Norfolk was twice the size of their previous town, David City. It was a railroad center between the Chicago, the North Western, and the Union Pacific lines.

Always eager and alert to finding new business opportunities, J. C. made sandwiches at home and sold them to the passengers. There were no dining cars on the train route, so business was good. There was a need, and he met it. Both businesses of selling lemonade and sandwiches were his first lessons about desires that consumers had for goods and services. (**Goods** *are things people can buy and use to satisfy wants; we can touch them.* **Services** *are activities people do for us, like giving haircuts.*) Perhaps at that age he had no idea what those economic terms meant. J. C. learned that when someone had a want (thirst or hunger) and was willing to pay the asked price, he had a sellable product. (**Wants** *are desires that can be satisfied by consuming goods and/or services.*)

(Dear Readers, Do you remember when there was a shortage of those furry, red creatures that would laugh when tickled? People would stand in line or even fight to buy one. Buyers will sometimes stand in line for hours, even camping out, to buy a particular computer component when there is a shortage. Sometimes there is a surplus. That means that people aren't willing to buy as much of a product at a particular price that a business wants to sell it for, or the product doesn't fulfill the needs of consumers.)

Chapter 2

Growing And Learning

While J. C. worked tirelessly at the bookstore, he received wages of eighteen dollars a month. (**Wages** *are the payments people receive for the work they provide.*) Even though it was a small amount, he was able to save some of it. *(To* **save** *is to put aside money for future use.)* He didn't spend much since he wasn't in the habit of spending all the money he earned. During the school months, he worked in the mornings and during the noon hour so his brothers could have lunch. He returned in the afternoon and worked until supper. After supper, he would return to work until 10:00 p.m. Remember, he was only eleven years old and in the sixth grade while keeping such a busy work schedule.

It was during that time when J. C. became interested in magazines. *American Magazine* was his favorite. The winter months gave him the opportunity to read the best-selling books. His favorite authors were Zane Grey and Mark Twain. The best-sellers for children were *Little Women, Black Beauty, and The Five Little Peppers and How They Grew.* Other favorites were books by Horatio Alger, who focused on people who were poor and became successful through hard work.

Magazines sold better than books, and cigar counters were the busiest part of any store. J. C. remembered that store owners would play dice poker with customers. The prize would be a cigar. It was a means, at the time, for promoting the selling of cigars.

J. C. recalled that white clay pipes were the most expensive. It was considered smart to polish the bowl of the pipe with the side of the nose. The oil in the skin would give the bowl a shine. People who smoked a corncob pipe were considered hicks, and only punks smoked cigarettes. Even at that time, cigarettes were referred to as a "coffin nail." Little was known then how true that saying would become today.

Selling candy was a profitable, demanding part of the brothers' business. J. C.'s job was to keep the plates well organized and full. William Werner, who owned a saloon, became one of their best customers in town. He came into the store every Saturday night and bought five dollars worth of candy for his three daughters. J. C. recalled that the effects of the candy didn't keep them from being attractive even while eating so many sweets—getting a round figure!

One winter night J. C. was attempting to kill a rat that he thought was invading the candy area. It turned out that the scratching was nothing more than a sad-faced, cold, and hungry little puppy. Because he was so small, J. C. tucked him into his coat sleeve and later carried him home. His mother wasn't happy about the new member of the family. He knew that he had a dog to keep, however, when she finally picked the dog up and cuddled him. The dog was named Teddy. He became a constant companion for many years. Teddy was named after President Theodore Roosevelt. It had become a popular name for children.

After several years of working hard and saving money, the family finally moved to a comfortable house with central heat and an indoor bathroom. Most of the time, Rollie was on the road selling candy. Always looking for ways to expand his business experiences and opportunities, J. C. took on an extra job selling newspapers. Buying a newspaper on Saturday night became a social event for the town's people. They would arrive by horse and buggy or they'd walk to town. Customers would parade up and down the street visiting with each other while eagerly waiting for the newspapers to arrive. The *Chicago American* had begun a comic section in their Sunday edition. That was in part why people were anxious to read the next episode. The store would stock four hundred copies and they'd sell out immediately.

The newspapers arrived at the Norfolk junction about a mile from the store. J. C. had to make several trips on his bike to bring them back to the store. It was on one such night that he learned that "a boy named Joyce," as well as being the newcomer to town, would be put in a position to defend his honor. One of the guys would mischievously entertain himself by jumping out from behind a tree, knocking over J. C. and the papers. That was just the beginning of his troubles with one of the town's bullies.

(Dear Readers, Have you ever had a problem with a bully in your school or in your neighborhood? How did you handle your situation? Did you ask an adult for help? Do you think most bullies are brave or cowards when confronted? Sometimes bullying can be verbal put-downs. Which types of bullying do you think are the worst—physical or verbal put-downs?)

One Saturday afternoon when he was scheduled to work in the bookstore by himself, J. C. ran quickly to the nearby restaurant for a sandwich. The same bully tripped J. C., and he fell flat on his face. J. C. jumped up and taught the bully a thing or two. Like most bullies, he was mainly talk. He never used J. C. as a scapegoat again.

The candy business was growing at such a fast rate that Rollie got to spend only one weekend a month at home. His sales areas were western Nebraska, Wyoming, and the Black Hills of South Dakota. Rollie took J. C., at the age of sixteen, with him so that the following summer, J. C. could take care of his sales territory. Rollie had never taken a vacation. He knew that if he did, he needed someone reliable to work his route. J. C. was proud to have been chosen as a summer replacement. It was during that time when J. C. observed how his older brother used his time wisely. The lesson was never forgotten and served J. C. well in the years ahead.

Since J. C. knew that going with Rollie would take them into some rough territories, he secretly took a .22 revolver with him. During a forty-mile trip with a mailman, they spotted some prairie chickens. J. C. pulled out his .22 and shot it. To his surprise, he hit one of the chickens. The most unexpected shock was when he learned that the mailman was also the game warden. Instead of arresting J. C. for not having a license to hunt, he joined the brothers in a prairie chicken dinner. It felt like he had gotten a lucky break until he received a stern tongue lashing from Rollie for bringing the gun.

While in training with Rollie, J. C. had his first encounter with Native Americans. He went with a local young man from the town of Chadron, Nebraska, to a reservation. There were around 3,000 Native Americans. His new friend spoke a mixture of English and Sioux to them. While observing their lifestyles, J. C. noticed a foul-smelling, dark substance hanging from the trees. It was his first knowledge that people ate dog meat. He was astonished that nothing was wasted by those Native Americans. They required very little for survival.

The following summer before J. C. set out to cover Rollie's territory, he got his first pair of long pants. Until then, his pants had come to his knees (called knickers), and the rest of his legs had been sometimes covered with long socks. J. C. was seventeen, and Rollie wanted him to look more like a man while he handled the candy route. J. C. would meet older clients and other salesmen. Most of the customers were Rollie's friends, so they were willing to give J. C. their orders. Some even gave him extra ones. It was during that experience when J. C. made the most crucial decision, up to this date of his life—his future was in SELLING.

Covering Rollie's candy route was not without incident or drama. One evening, J. C. was in Lander, Wyoming—a wild cow town. He rented a room on the first floor in the front of the building. Suddenly, he was awakened about midnight by rowdy cowpunchers. They were riding up and down the wooden walk shooting their six-shooters! He hit the floor almost as fast as the bullets went zinging over his head. In spite of those "grown-up" long pants, he didn't feel very brave!

(Dear Readers, Remember, this was still in the early 1900s. The west was anything but settled and civilized.)

Traveling on the train and an occasional stage coach was part of his exciting summer. It was almost like a party, as the salesmen would swap stories, and shoot dice. He was pleased that he could add to the stories with his Wyoming adventure. It was quite a learning experience for such a young man—not only successfully handling his brother's candy route but being totally accepted by the older salesmen.

Upon returning to Norfolk, Rollie gave J. C. a hunting-case pocket watch. It was an expensive one for the time—worth about forty-five dollars. J. C. cherished that gift for many years. The watch symbolized a gift from an admired brother who had become his friend and mentor.

That fall, when the Rosebud Indian Reservation was open to settlers, two trains were scheduled to come through Norfolk every night for a week. Seizing another new business opportunity, J. C. sold popcorn. He popped and sacked all the popcorn he could carry. It sold out almost immediately! He had just enough time to go back and return with more popcorn before the second train came through.

The second night, he got help and pushed a popcorn wagon to the junction. When the first train arrived, he was well supplied. On one such evening, he made a profit of $80. **(Profit** *is the money remaining after all costs of production are paid. Profit is income for entrepreneurs.)* His main operating expenses—the cost to sell the popcorn—were the popcorn wagon, popcorn, and butter. The three items had been bought for a good price. After selling popcorn for several nights, J. C. managed to earn $180.00.

(Dear Readers, This is an important dollar amount for you to remember, because that money led to another business venture that changed his life. Remember the term "opportunity recognition.")

Chapter 3

Going To Kansas City

One evening as J. C. worked alone in the bookstore, a very stylish looking man wandered in and wanted to speak to the owner. Little did J. C. know that this would be the second important milestone in his life—becoming a salesman had been the first decision.

Upon being told that the proprietors were not present, the salesman decided to pass the time talking to J. C. (**Proprietor(s)** *are one or more who owns or shares in ownership of a business.*) It turned out that the salesman represented a large importer of postcards. The cards were bright and larger than the cards presently used. In those days, people usually didn't throw received cards away. They would keep them in an album much like the baseball and football cards collected today.

The gentleman had come from Chicago and was looking for someone interested in having a wholesale business selling his cards. (**Wholesale** *is the selling of goods in large quantities to be retailed by others.*) The sales pitch was that some of his wholesalers had been very successful selling his cards—even in small towns. Rollie was out of town with his candy territory. His brother Bill was the only one around to discuss the matter. J. C.'s mission was to sell him on the idea. He proposed to Bill that he would use the $180 made from the popcorn business. Bill and Rollie would match the same amount. That would give them $540 of venture capital. (**Venture capital** *is the money needed to start a business.*) Bill was not impressed with the new idea!

Nevertheless, the next morning, Bill and the salesman discussed the matter. After two hours, Bill was convinced that selling postcards at the wholesale level would expand their business. (*Dear Readers, Entrepreneurs who wish to grow must seek new business opportunities or ways to better use their time and money. Food chains change their menus to keep customers satisfied and interested. Can you think of a new product added to a business where you buy any goods or services? J. C. was experiencing an important characteristic of an entrepreneur known as* opportunity recognition. **Opportunity recognition** *is the ability to see the potential of a new idea or product.)*

J. C. named the new firm the Norfolk Postcard Company. The business plan was that they would get other salesmen to sell the postcards on their routes—the same way Rollie sold candy. Soon, half a dozen salespeople were doing well. Once again, it took some persuading for J. C. to convince Rollie and Bill that he could sell the cards after school on Fridays. He could expand their sales further by going to other towns on Saturdays. Within a brief time, the card company began making a profit, since none of the three brothers was drawing a salary. *(Dear Readers, Wages are a part of business expenses. As entrepreneurs, the brothers agreed not to take a salary for themselves but to put all of the money back into the business. They bought only the essentials for living.)*

In August 1909, J. C. met with a surprise while going with Rollie to Omaha, Nebraska, on the candy route. Rollie had arranged for the two of them to have a meeting with their father. They had not seen him for ten years, and by then, their mother had divorced George Hall. A brief time later, after the reunion with their father, George Hall left Nebraska to live in California—leaving his family behind. They never saw him again.

There had been discussions from time to time about selling the bookstore and moving to a larger city, and Omaha, Nebraska, had been one of their choices. The brothers ended their partnership with Mr. Jay. They weren't sure there was much of an opportunity for growth in the small town of Norfolk—but an unforeseen opportunity occurred that caught J. C's attention.

It was in December 1909 when a cigar salesman from Kansas City, Missouri entered J. C. Hall's life. What impressed J. C. so much was that the gentleman kept talking about the "Kansas City Spirit." The salesman said that even in the midst of setbacks for the city, Kansas City always arose to any situation and moved forward. He reminded J. C. that Kansas City was centrally located in the United States. Railroads made it a perfect wholesale and distribution center. J. C. had long understood the value of the railroad systems.

After much begging, disapproval, and conversation, J. C. finally convinced his family of the practical wisdom for him to make the move alone. The selling points were that moving had already been discussed, and he had promised to go to school. On January 9, 1910, he left Norfolk with a one-way ticket to Kansas City, Missouri. *(Dear Readers, This might be a good time to look at a map and locate Kansas City, Missouri, as well as observing the states surrounding that area.)*

Y. M. C. A. BLDG., KANSAS CITY, MO.   5855

Kansas City YMCA, the first "headquarters" for J. C. Hall.

When J. C. arrived at the old Union Station at the age of eighteen, the frigid weather, and what seemed to be cold people as well, added to his overwhelming feelings of loneliness, even though he was in a city of 250,000 people. *(Dear Readers, Have you ever had the feeling of being alone even when you were surrounded by people? Perhaps you had a parent who left, or someone died, or maybe you suffered some form of abuse.)*

Since the fare to the YMCA in a horse-drawn cab was too expensive, J. C. walked to his first home and office. It was a corner room on the top floor and measured 12 × 12 or 144 square feet. His office would actually be the space under his bed where he placed the two shoe boxes filled with postcards.

After getting settled, he decided there was no time like the present to explore the city. It might help take away his loneliness. J. C. had a hearty breakfast and bought a much needed overcoat and a new pair of shoes—those items would be called "goods." The next task was a haircut. The barber told him he was going to give him such a good cut that he'd come back. He did—for almost fifty years. Remember the word "services?

1910, the year that J. C. arrived in Kansas City.

To keep his promise, the next morning, J. C. registered at Spalding's Commercial College. He enrolled in commercial law, penmanship, and spelling. A sign tacked between the first and second floors read, "Time is money—save time." Although the sign had meaning to J. C. because of his experiences of saving time that first summer with Rollie, he changed some of the words to, "Time is everything—save time." Adopting this slogan motivated J. C. to never sit around and wait for things to happen. He committed himself to making things happen! That's exactly what he did his entire life!

J. C. created his first written business plan. *(A* **business plan** *is a document an entrepreneur prepares that describes his or her product, cost, competition, and marketing plan; a formal statement of a company's goals and strategy to achieve them—a road map.)* An important part of the plan was to analyze the territory. J. C. had been thinking of a mail-order business. He had to research the towns with a population of 1,000 but less than 10,000 near Kansas City. The cards came in packages of one hundred. He had to separate them and repackage them for mailing. No proprietor would want one hundred cards with the same design.

The invoices, printed by one of the printers in Kansas City, were a novel invention. "Kansas City Branch" (even if it was a shoebox under his bed) was printed as the home address. Norfolk was the branch office. One of the women in the printing shop suggested using her brother's Broadway address, which gave them a New York office.

(Dear Readers, An invoice is a list of goods sent or services performed, as well as prices and charges. When teachers order something for their classrooms, they have to give an invoice to the school office. It is a record of what they ordered. When a car is repaired, the garage gives an invoice listing the parts that were replaced as well as the labor costs.)

One hundred cards plus an invoice would be sent to "the leading postcard dealer" in every town. Some post offices would ask for money for return postage. There was no such person in some towns. Others kept the cards and didn't pay for them. The more honest ones kept the cards, paid for them, and wanted more to sell. Using such a system of trial and error gave J. C. quite a list of customers. The young entrepreneur began making a profit. Within months, J. C. had pinched and saved $200.00. He was ready to open up a business account at the First National Bank.

The increase in business was not without challenges—the little room and postcard business became a problem for the YMCA. The post office didn't like handling all the packages in one small mailbox. The solution for this problem was to rent a room in the Braley Building for an office with storage space. The mail-order business grew. J. C. began to spend three or four days working in nearby towns.

By fall, J. C. couldn't afford to go back to school due to time management. If he didn't devote his time to business, he could lose it altogether. The small business was no longer a sideline, and more space was needed. He rented an adjoining room in the same building. His family understood his reasons for not returning to school.

He made another new business decision to print some of the cards himself and added quotes by famous men. Another thought was that printing and making his own products allowed him to control the quality. It became important for him to send the very best to the consumers. (**Consumers** *are those who use goods or services.*)

Being the wise, young businessman that J. C. had become, he realized that postcards were not the best way for people to communicate. No personal notes could be written. Anyone could read them. He knew that another product would soon replace the postcards.

Between thoughts of new product development and hard work, J. C. found time to enjoy the theater as well as other sights and sounds. Kansas City had the best theaters between Chicago and San Francisco. He and his friends would buy twenty-five cent tickets in the second section. Some of the favorite performers were Eddie Cantor, the Marx Brothers, and Lillian Russell. His love for the theater grew. On an occasional business trip to New York, when times got much better, he enjoyed a few Broadway shows. He enjoyed the usual sightseeing. It didn't include the Empire State Building. (*Dear Readers, Do you know when the Empire State Building was built?*)

Kansas City was in a huge period of growth. Motion pictures were starting. Open park concerts brought the likes of John Philip Sousa, a famous music writer for bands. There was an amusement park like a miniature Disneyland. Walt Disney was living in Kansas City also. In the later years when they became friends, J. C. teased Disney that he got the idea for his amusement parks in Kansas City.

With the excitement of all the growth, the Kansas City Spirit had become a part of J. C.'s life. He knew he wanted to stay. Within a year, he finally convinced his mother, Rollie, and Marie to join him. They bought a comfortable house on Troost Avenue. A long year of being alone had ended. Being alone had been one of the greatest opportunity costs that J. C. had experienced since moving away from home. (**Opportunity costs** *are the highest value alternative given up when a choice is made.*) Later in his life, J. C. evaluated being away from his family as a greater cost than he had recognized at the time.

(*Dear Readers, All of us face opportunity costs with every decision-choice that we make when more choices are given. An example is when you might have to decide whether to study for a test or take a lower grade. Perhaps you have had to decide whether to tell someone the truth about a matter or you tried to get away with something by telling a lie. What you gave up is the cost or the forgone alternative. Sometimes while making choices or decisions, some of the criteria of what we want will have to be traded. An example would be when you want a particular pair of jeans, and you have to give up the exact style because of the color or price. You may hear someone say that it was a trade-off.*)

Chapter 4

Building An Unknown Future

For the next two years, Rollie and J. C. didn't receive wages. Money, again, was spent only for necessities. The sales philosophies that they both agreed on were never to use pressure—to sell only a product that they believed in—to never sell anything to a dealer that they didn't feel they could sell themselves. J. C. didn't see the business ever growing with just the two of them selling. Rollie once again believed in J. C.'s idea of hiring more salesmen on a commission basis. (*A* **commission** *is a part or income from what an individual sells).* The idea was financed with long-term credit. *(***Long-term credit** *is when you have a longer period of time to repay money borrowed, usually at a lower interest rate, such as when buying a house.)*

Rollie went out for two or three weeks to cover the most productive business towns just as he had done with the candy business. J. C. worked the areas closest to home. At twenty years of age, he bought his first car. It was a Hupmobile, a low-priced car. A Prestolite tank on the running board furnished gas for the headlights. The taillight burned coal oil. Since few roads were paved, he drove mostly in Missouri gumbo-mud! Often a farmer had to pull him out of the sticky mud. Tires were no better. On a trip to St. Louis, he had to stop and change tires eighteen times. Only such a daring young man would think that sort of an automobile would be fun. That car became one of the reasons his business was growing.

By 1911, they had rented the entire third floor of a warehouse. J. C. thought that the space would be adequate for many years. He and Rollie worked six days a week, from 7:00 in the morning until 6:00 at night.

Almost a year later, J. C.'s previous concern about the quantity demand of the postcard business began to become a reality. *(***Quantity demand** *is the amount of products or services that people are willing and able to buy at a certain price.)* Cheaper cards were being manufactured. The public was having less and less to do with postcards. The brothers decided to add Valentine cards to their stock, and many were sent in envelopes. People were beginning to buy greeting cards of the highest quality. However, the term "greeting cards" was not used during those early years. Instead, cards were given the names of just "Easter cards" or "Christmas cards."

Rollie and J. C. added leather postcards, using a hot plate to burn in the design. The largest selling card had a bold-typed message that said, "Smile, damn you, smile." During those painful and exhausting years of poverty and building a business, J. C. found that his life had few light moments and fewer smiles.

Another design that J. C. identified with was, "When you get to the end of your rope, tie a knot in it, and hang on." In the years that followed, there were times when it was all he could do to hang on!

(Dear Readers, When you look at the success of such a great company like Hallmark, it is sometimes difficult to understand the hardships that can come with building a business. The vision of success looks easy and glamorous to those of us looking on now. You might want to interview a business person in your town and ask if he or she has a story about "hanging on" in that business venture.)

Rollie and J. C.'s direct and honest ways of dealing with their dealers continued. Both would give advice about what would sell and what wouldn't. They took poor-selling cards out of the line. J. C.'s sales records were all in his head. The only thing on paper was what people owed them.

Knowing what sells and what doesn't sell is a small part of what is referred to as **product research** and J. C. was excellent at it. During those formative years, their recordkeeping was the groundwork for today's business. Cards and products were rated according to what should be continued and what should be dropped. That method of recordkeeping was revolutionary at the time. The common idea was to sell any way you could, regardless of quality. The Hall brothers never embraced such a selling scheme.

In 1914, a retail store became their next step for more progress in the card enterprise. Added to the first store were items like calendars and children's books. By now, the brothers knew that postcards had had their day of popularity. *(Dear Readers, A retail store gave them hands-on product research. They had to skillfully select items to sell. Retail businesses have continued to be an important part of the Hallmark company.)*

A new business challenge occurred when, without any notice, their card suppliers, Murray Engraving Company, directed a salesman to tell the Hall brothers that they wanted only to sell retail, and not wholesale, to them. The cost for the cards, and the price they would have to charge for them, would be more than the consumers would be willing to pay. The cost of production would give them far less profit. It would put their business in jeopardy!

J. C. went to an engraving company in Kansas City to see if they would engrave cards for Christmas sales. They consented to engrave a poinsettia, a holly wreath, a vase with roses, and two others. It gave them a line of twenty cards.

Because of the small "runs" (the total amount of cards printed), the cards were not profitable. It was the **first time,** however, that their name was on a card—"Published by Hall Bros., Kansas City, MO, Made in U.S.A." It was the beginning of being publishers!

(Dear Readers, Did you know that if a retail business doesn't make most of their sales during the Christmas holiday, it is often not going to make enough money to stay in business or support slower months? Next holiday, listen to the news about how well businesses are doing in their sales. It is crucial.)

Another major challenge to hit their business came in 1915. A newly shipped supply of Valentine cards was lost due to a fire. It would have been the perfect time to quit! *(Dear Readers, Remember the saying "tying a knot, and hanging on?" This was definitely one of those times. They were shocked but not whipped. Can you think of a time when you felt that way? Perhaps you know someone or have read another book about a famous person who was successful in spite of their hardships. I'm sure you have heard of Dr. Martin Luther King or Gandhi. Can you imagine today calling suppliers for new inventory and telling them you don't know how you're going to be able to pay them? That is exactly what J. C. did!)*

There was no inventory, and Valentine's Day was a large retail day. (**Inventory** *is a detailed list of goods, supplies, and materials in stock in a company or store.)* It all had been destroyed in the fire except for the safe. By ten o'clock the next day, suppliers were sending shipments by express. The $9,000 insurance policy didn't cover the entire loss. J. C. estimated that they were starting over with "$17,000 behind scratch." That meant starting lower than they had been at the beginning of their company's formation!

It was during that time when the "Kansas City Spirit" spoke kindly to the Hall brothers, when a gentleman named Willard Rupe offered them space without a charge. Mr. Rupe furnished them a typewriter, tables, and chairs. The brothers occupied the space for several years. Rent was paid every month even though Mr. Rupe offered them the room rent free. His generous offer was enough encouragement for them to continue.

That same year, when the Smith-Pierce Engraving Company was in financial trouble, the Hall brothers assumed the debts of their six presses and began experimenting with their own cards. They engraved new dies for Christmas cards and hired several women who added hand coloring. (Dies are carved to cut the same shape every time they are pressed. Teachers often use dies to cut out letters or shapes.) They had gone from being salesmen, to being wholesalers, to being publishers, and then to being manufacturers. It had been a year of disasters that ended on a high note.

(Dear Readers, Remember when we spoke earlier about how entrepreneurs must always look for new business opportunities or ways to expand their operations? Manufacturing was the beginning of a new expansion for the Hall brothers. It gave them more control over quantity and quality. They didn't have to depend on an engraving company to supply them with their cards.)

New products continued to filter into the retail store—sometimes by accident! Gift wrapping or "gift dressing" was plain white, red, and green tissue paper and one holly pattern. During the Christmas season of 1917, after selling the entire supply of wrapping paper, Rollie found some fancy decorated envelope lining paper as a replacement. The paper sold so fast that one would have thought that customers were at a half-price sale. The following year, the paper was sold in packages of three, and again they sold out. The scarcity of the gift dressing led to a new product idea. (**Scarcity** *is the condition that occurs when people's wants for goods and services are greater than the resources available.*) Gift wrapping paper was their **first** departure from greeting cards.

(Dear Readers, This was just the beginning for Hall Brothers' varied line of products. If you don't believe it, visit a Hallmark Gold Crown® store today and notice the many products they sell that go beyond greeting cards.)

When one of the major card suppliers was going out of business, J. C. called to ask if they could buy their manufacturing equipment. Mr. Bergman, the owner, invited him to New York to discuss the matter. Bergman startled J. C. when he offered the equipment to him below the appraised value. That manufacturing equipment would increase their assets from six machines to twenty-six. Furthermore, Mr. Bergman put no deadline on the note, and didn't charge interest! (**Interest** *is the price paid for using someone else's money.*)

(Dear Readers, You may be wondering why Mr. Bergman would make such an arrangement. I forgot to tell you that once when J. C. was looking over an invoice, he noticed that a sizeable amount had been left off—eighteen hundred dollars! It was a difficult wrestling match with his conscience—what to do. Knowing that he couldn't live with it, J. C. sent the money owed.

The opportunity cost was to keep it or send it. Bergman never forgot—you decide! A bit of advice: common interest, at a fair rate, is usually paid by consumers getting a loan for a house, car, or business. The highest interest paid is most commonly on a credit card debt. Remember, the use of a credit card is a loan! Just think, a $50.00 pair of jeans could cost as much as $150.00 if the credit card bill was not paid in full. The high interest quickly adds to the final price.)

Larger varieties of everyday cards were becoming popular. A few examples were birth announcements, birthdays, weddings, anniversaries, illness, and sympathy. Seasonal cards were Christmas, Halloween, St. Patrick's Day, Thanksgiving, Father's Day, and Mother's Day. Cards expressing friendship were added in 1919.

J. C. saw greeting cards as a way to help people express their feelings. He appreciated the value of privacy when one bought a card to send in an envelope—unlike the postcards. Some have credited the Hallmark company with the beginning of the modern greeting card business. The idea of greetings, however, goes back as far as the ancient Egyptians and the Greeks. Those first greetings were written on scrolls (rolled up messages) or on papyrus. Some books of the Bible are referred to as greetings or poems.

It soon became apparent that if growth were to continue, the Hall brothers had to expand to the eastern part of the country. New York was the most important place to start. A salesman by the name of Harry Lange was recommended to J. C. to run that section. J. C. was not comfortable with the Brooklyn accent and mannerisms. He didn't want to hire Lange. However, J. C. agreed to meet with him the next day for the second time. Surprisingly, he hired him. Mr. Lange proved to be just the man to handle the tough buyers of New York.

Later, one of the men that Harry Lange hired moved to California to open that area. By 1922, there were sixteen salesmen doing business in all forty-eight states. *(Dear Readers, Do you know why all fifty states were not included on the list of the states?)*

Business grew faster than they could find trained personnel. The company's reputation brought good people to work for them. When there was a need to move to a new factory location, the employees voted on which location they preferred. The new location meant no affordable places to eat. A company cafeteria was opened—another new idea, at the time, for any company!

By now, Bill had sold the book and stationery store in Norfolk, Nebraska, and moved his family to Kansas City. The Hall brothers expanded to three. All the space in the new building was filled. The 144-square-foot business space first used in the YMCA room had grown to 60,000 square feet.

During that period of progress, the name Hall evolved to become ***Hallmark***. Mr. Hall had read about how in the fourteenth century in London, the goldsmiths put a mark guaranteeing the purity of the gold and silver articles they made. It was called a "hall mark." Combining the family name and the word "mark" seemed a natural way to signify quality for their products. By 1928, the Hallmark brand name was being used on the backs of all cards.

New leases gave them 75,000 square feet by 1929, which was also the year that the first logo, a torch and shield, was adopted to signify the company. *(A* **logo** *is a symbol used by a company or business as an emblem.)*

(Dear Reader, You possibly have a logo on something you are wearing today. Do you like to wear clothing items with a certain logo? Have you ever thought of it as giving free advertising to a company? What about electronic products? I know that you have seen golden arches, a check mark, or an apple that represents companies. The marketing reason for this is so those items or places of business are easily identified—often without words.)

At one time, there had been some conversation about moving the company east. An exploratory trip east brought them right back to Kansas City. It would be difficult to duplicate the organization they had built. The quality of the environment and the people making quality products were the main factors for staying. Besides, why would they want to leave the "Kansas City Spirit?"

Chapter 5

Economic Changes and New Growth

During the Depression in the 1930s, the company was hit hard like everyone else. There was fear that people would stop buying greeting cards because of the scarcity of money. Mr. Hall felt that greeting cards would be substituted for gifts, since consumers found themselves with the need to make the best economic choices.

*(Dear Readers, An example of **substitutes** is when people buy orange juice in place of apple juice. Substitutes prompt the drive for the advertisements you see printed or on the television. Companies spend an enormous amount of money because of substitutes—trying to prove that their product is the "best choice." Sometimes famous people are used so that consumers can relate to them as a user of a particular product—like athletic shoes!)*

Against the advice of all concerned, Mr. Hall refused to lay off a single employee because of the Depression. The employees voted not to have anyone laid off but to reduce their salaries by 10 percent. In time, full pay was restored. Another economic crisis was solved by discussing the problem with the employees.

While looking after new territories, Mr. Hall became aware of the way greeting cards were not consistently being displayed or in a way that made them easy to browse. Cards were displayed on flat counters. Others were left in drawers. Some dealers used metal racks. He remembered standing in a store and seeing that greeting cards made the worst showing of any product. He knew there needed to be a change.

In 1935, an architectural designer was hired to build a new display so the cards could be easily seen with less difficulty and in the open. Simply, people could get to them freely without having to ask. The result was the Eye-Vision patented fixture. *(A **patent** is a document that gives a company or inventor the sole rights to sell or use an invention for a limited period of time.)* It was the slanted fixtures that you see today when buying a greeting card. The company agreed to sell the fixtures at cost to their dealers. However, the drawback was that salesmen couldn't generate an interest by showing a photo. The solution was that a trailer was built to carry the installed fixtures with a model display of greeting cards. By 1939, the fixtures were selling themselves. Dealers' businesses didn't just show an increase in sales—they doubled and sometimes tripled!

New products and advertising were created that included the first Disney card. The pansy card was introduced in 1939 as a Mother's Day card. It became the most popular card made by Hallmark—over 30,000,000 have been sold!

In 1939, the popular Chicago-based "Tony Wons Radio Show" was sponsored by the company. Tony encouraged the listeners to look on the back of the Hallmark card. When Tony Wons joined NBC radio in 1940, it marked the beginning of the time in which the Hall Brothers gained national visibility in the marketplace.

During the forties, the company adopted the slogan, "When You Care Enough to Send the Very Best." *(A **slogan** is a short phrase used in a company's advertising.)* It was penned by one of the employees, Ed Goodman. It became a standard for the Hallmark company. Their slogan is possibly one of the most well-known in advertising.

Ed Goodman

The five-point crown replaced the torch and shield as the company's trademark. *(Dear Readers, In 1949, the Hallmark logo as you know it today became the* registered trademark.*) (A* **trademark** *is a manufacturer's or trader's registered emblem or the name that identifies his/her goods.)* It is the ***crown*** and ***Hallmark signature*** that is seen on all of the company's products. Andrew Szoeke, an artist and designer, worked with staff artists to create the logo.

The Hallmark trademark today—the crown with Hallmark under it.

The enormous growth prompted the Hall brothers to build two new facilities in Topeka and Lawrence, Kansas. The dream became a reality—Hallmark was producing one million cards a day.

Rollie, Bill, and Mr. Hall continued to build the business together. There were a few good times for relaxation. Their mother didn't live to see her sons build the business to the success it was enjoying by now. She had vowed to see her sons grow up, and she did. She was always interested in their lives and saw a hopeful future for them. She died at the young age of fifty-six from cancer. Mr. Hall remembered her life as one of giving. Years later, when the business grew to mammoth proportions, her three sons honored her by building the Nancy Dudley Hall Laboratory of Mammalian Genetics at the University of Kansas—her life continued giving through the research.

Chapter 6

Mr. Hall and His Family

(Dear Readers, We have spent some time now looking at the development and growth of Hallmark Cards, Inc. For me, it is a good time to take a break from business and look at Mr. Hall's personal life. He had a life other than business—well, almost!)

Mr. Hall credits the event of meeting his bride, Elizabeth Ann Dilday, as a change for the better. It was about the time that Mr. Hall had bought a new sports car, a Stutz, for $600.00. Elizabeth was a good friend of his sister, Marie. J. C. took Marie to visit Elizabeth and her two-year-old niece, Lucy Jean. Meeting little Lucy Jean was love at first sight for Mr. Hall. His love for Elizabeth came later! It was the beginning of the ritual of taking the three of them for rides when he could find some spare time. Even when Lucy Jean went home, he found extra time to take Elizabeth for rides!

Not long after Lucy Jean returned to her home in Arkansas, she became very ill. Elizabeth was summoned to help her. After what seemed a very short time, Elizabeth notified Mr. Hall that Lucy had died. She asked that Mr. Hall give the bad news to Lucy Jean's grandmother. It was the most personal, and difficult task he had ever faced. Elizabeth stayed with her sister for a long period of mourning.

The loss of the young child brought Mr. Hall and Elizabeth closer. They found that they shared many things in common. They enjoyed automobile trips, horseback riding, and the theater. He teased her that she liked his automobile the best. However, when Mr. Hall proposed to Elizabeth, she accepted.

They married and settled down in Kansas City, and eventually bought a house on forty-one acres. Their first child, a daughter, Elizabeth Ann, was born on July 8, 1922. Their second child, Barbara Louise, was born on October 21, 1923. Donald Joyce Hall, their only son, was born on July 9, 1928. The family wanted to name him Joyce, but Mr. Hall didn't want his child having the same battles he'd had with a girl's name. He compromised and allowed Joyce to be his son's middle name.

Elizabeth's mother was living with them, and Rollie spent most of his weekends there. They soon felt the need to add on to the house. After much planning, it seemed more desirable to build a new, and bigger one. Since they were too far out of town for fire protection, the construction of the house took careful planning. It was a Georgian style, built of concrete and steel, and had a stone and brick exterior. In time, the house sat on six hundred acres as Mr. Hall expanded the acreage around it.

Summers in the Midwest proved to be their usual hot temperatures and full of humidity. Going to Colorado to escape the weather seemed a logical solution. After the Hall's put an ad in the *Denver Post*, a man sent them a picture of a Swiss chalet–style house overlooking the Grand Lake. They liked it so well that they later became owners instead of renters.

Rollie visited them and taught his brother how to trout fish. In fact, he returned for twenty-five summers to fish with Mr. Hall. One evening they stayed out too late to find their way back to the house. It became dark quickly in the mountains when the sun went down. Luckily, they had their German shepherd named Del Masco with them. They tied a fish line to him and kept yelling, "Go home, Masco. Go home." It took an hour for Del Masco to find their way back home.

It was during one of the visits to the mountains that Del Masco met with a terrible accident. He would walk in front of Elizabeth, who fed him every day. It was dark, and he heard a noise in the brush. Wanting to protect Elizabeth, he attacked what was later found to be a porcupine. He was shot full of quills. In spite of the family spending the night removing the quills, Del Masco died the next day on the vet's examining table.

(Dear Readers, Do you know why the porcupine quills had such a devastating effect on Del Masco? Was the porcupine simply trying to defend itself?)

The Hall children grew up liking the artwork and the new ideas that their father brought home. Elizabeth was equally interested in her husband's business and became an expert in the greeting card business. The family even spent time together going around the company's territories. Their car would be shipped by train to the area, and the family would ride the same train. (Shipping a car then cost a little more than for a passenger.)

Donald J. Hall was introduced to the greeting business at an early age, and grew up wanting to be part of his father's company. He became a sales trainee and worked as a sales representative while attending Dartmouth College. After graduation and a tour of duty with the Army, he joined the company as assistant to the president in 1953. Being the boss's son was not easy, because his mistakes were noticed more than those of anyone else in the company. Donald never created problems for his dad. Donald Hall was named President and Chief Executive Officer of Hallmark Cards, Inc. in 1966.

(Dear Readers, Although the goal of this biography is to inform my readers about the magnificent life of Mr. J. C. Hall, more will be written about the success of Mr. Donald Hall and his contributions to Hallmark. The influence and dreams of his father allowed him to continue the growth and development of the company. Today, the company is led by the third generation of the Hall family—two of Mr. J. C. Hall's grandsons—Donald J. Hall Jr. is President and CEO, and David E. Hall is President of Hallmark's personal expression group overseeing the wholesale business.)

One proud statistic that Mr. Hall enjoyed telling about his family was that he and Elizabeth had fifty-five years together. They shared three children, eleven grandchildren, and even great-grandchildren. Family, even in Mr. Hall's formative years with his mother, brothers, and sister, had long been among his most cherished assets and blessings—even more than business.

Chapter 7

Progress of New Ideas

The first presidential Christmas cards were printed by Hallmark in 1953 for President and Mrs. Dwight D. Eisenhower. The card showed a portrait of Abraham Lincoln that President Eisenhower had painted himself. Thank you cards were produced for Mrs. Eisenhower as well. Hallmark has continued to print Christmas cards for most presidents and some vice presidents since that first order.

Radio was the most popular means of communication in 1948 when the "Hallmark Playhouse" presented shows. Later, Hallmark went from asking people to listen to productions on the radio to looking at what they could see through television. Some of the great actors and actresses of that time who played in those productions were Helen Hayes, Julie Harris, Mary Martin, Charles Boyer, Peter Ustinov, and Richard Chamberlain.

Those early television specials were the beginning of the "Hallmark Hall of Fame." The first production in December 1951, *Amahl and the Night Visitors,* was an opera created for television. It was presented as a Hallmark Hall of Fame production seven times, from 1951 to 1965.

Amahl and the Night Vistors

Picture of Mr. J. C. Hall with Hallmark's first Emmy

In 1953, Shakespeare's *Hamlet* was presented. An Emmy for those first-rate television productions was presented almost ten years later to Mr. J. C. Hall by the National Academy of Television Arts and Sciences. It was the first Emmy ever given to a sponsor. Hallmark has continued to receive many Emmys since the first one. It was during that same year that Her Majesty Queen Elizabeth II named Mr. J. C. Hall an Honorary Commander of the Order of the British Empire.

For years, Mr. J. C. Hall had bought property around the company's headquarters. At the time he made the purchases, he didn't have in mind what would later become the bridge between his company and downtown Kansas City.

The vision of a place called Crown Center, after the symbol of Hallmark, began in 1968. The first long construction program was not completed until 1973. It was a four hundred million dollar project on eighty-five acres. Mr. Hall's intent was to bring people back to the city by building a first-class project in the middle of Kansas City, instead of going out to the meadows and fields of the suburbs. Surrounded by garden plazas, walkways, and fountains,

Crown Center presently houses office complexes, hotels, a retail center, and a variety of restaurants. It also includes high-rise apartments and condominiums. Development and refinement of the complex continues as new office buildings are added, as well as stores and restaurants.

Although Crown Center was the dream of Mr. J. C. Hall, his son, Donald J. Hall, became responsible for the reality and completion of his father's ideas. It was not an easy task. In the spirit of his father's work ethic, Donald Hall took the dream further than Mr. J. C. Hall had ever visualized. Crown Center has been compared to an ancient marketplace like the Forum in Rome, Italy. To Mr. J. C. Hall, it was an area where people could come in the midst of art, food, shopping, and they could enjoy a fine gathering place. It certainly was unlike the gathering of people when Mr. Hall sold newspapers at his brother's bookstore. Perhaps that is where the dream began.

Mr. J. C. Hall and Donald looking at a model of Crown Center

Kaleidoscope, part of Crown Center, has been inspiring creativity in kids since 1969. On a daily basis, children come to have an artistic experience making "something" out of materials that would normally be discarded from Hallmark's manufacturing process. Since Crayola® is a subsidiary of the Hallmark company, children find an abundance of markers and crayons. Children visiting Kansas City are invited to come to this area of Crown Center. Reservations are encouraged due to the large crowds. As of September 2007, Kaleidoscope has given more than 6.8 million children the opportunity to flex their creative muscles and make art. The Hallmark Visitors Center, next to Kaleidoscope, houses the timeline, historical displays, and interactive exhibits of Hallmark Cards, Inc.

During his life, Mr. J. C. Hall had the privilege of meeting many famous people, either through using their talents in the Hallmark company, or through mutual friends. These included Presidents Eisenhower and Truman, as well as Sir Winston Churchill, Prime Minister of England. In fact, the Hall family visited Sir Winston Churchill at his home several times. It was there that Mr. Hall first saw Sir Winston Churchill's paintings.

After much persuading, Sir Winston Churchill signed a three-year contract with Hallmark to allow the reproduction of a limited number of his paintings for cards. Mr. Hall was greatly honored when one of Sir Winston Churchill's original paintings was presented to him. It was placed in Mr. Hall's office.

Mr. Hall looking at paintings by Sir. Winston Churchill.

Many other talented artists' works has been used on Hallmark cards. Artists like Walt Disney, Norman Rockwell, Grandma Moses, Charles Schulz, Georgia O'Keefe, Andrew Wyeth, Pablo Picasso, and old masters like Michelangelo and Leonardo da Vinci have graced the front of greeting cards.

Hallmark gave a lot of attention not only to the graphics but to the messages on their cards. The philosophy was that the graphics first attract a customer, but it is the message that sells the card. Research had shown that during the early years of writing for greeting cards, buyers preferred verse to prose. Verse is described as a more romantic language; it rhymes—it forms a poem. Prose is the opposite and does not rhyme. Today people prefer a shorter, more conversational style of prose. Messages are usually written by the Hallmark staff. Writers like Ogden Nash, Norman Vincent Peale, Fulton Sheen, Maya Angelou, and the great literary works of Shakespeare, Charles Dickens, Walt Whitman, John Keats, Mark Twain, and Ralph Waldo Emerson have been used as messages.

Even in the midst of all the designs and great writers, one of the amusing stories of the production of a card happened when one of the greeting cards had a misspelled word on it. The card was meant to read, "Congratulations on Your New Venture." Instead it read, "Congratulations on Your New Denture."

When producing a greeting card, the artists and writers are just part of the process. A large staff may be involved. It is called division of labor. *(****Division of labor*** *occurs when people specialize in one task of a production process. The people who do mental and/or physical work in our economy are the* **human resources.***)* "At any given time, Hallmark employees are "inventing, creating, consulting, writing, designing, illustrating, editing, photographing, testing, revising, producing, casting, printing, shipping, and selling." Today, this division of labor is shared by 16,000 Hallmark employees worldwide.

Hallmark cards may be flocked, flittered, coated, dyed, glued, laminated, embossed, die cut, engraved, and glossed. They may be treated to look like leather, suede wood, satin, cloth, or metal. They may be permeated with oil, wood grain, cellulose fibers, colored threads, or diamond-dust sequins! If the right paper can't be found, they create it. If the right ink can't be found, they make it.

(Dear Readers, Many of the procedures listed are examples of the use of **natural** *or* **capital resources***. Wood and oil are examples of natural resources. Remember the manufacturing equipment that Mr. Hall bought from Mr. Bergman? That is one example of capital resources. Have you ever worked on a project with other people to create something or to complete an assignment? Was your strategy to divide the work*

so that each individual could use his or her best talents? Do you like assignments that require working with a group? That is what is meant when division of labor is used in a production process. Each individual does one specific, specialized part. Think of all of the people it takes to build one automobile.)

The idea of it taking the talents of many people to bring about the success of Hallmark Cards, Inc. is why the company has grown to the size that it is today. Even in the beginning, Mr. J. C. Hall went to those individuals who were willing to give their best to accomplish a goal. The patented Eye-Vision fixture is one example of using the talents of qualified individuals. Another important example was hiring Harry Lange to expand the team of salesmen. Recall the artists and writers who have been named.

Today, nearly one hundred years later, Hallmark's world headquarters remains in Kansas City, Missouri. In the United States, more than 3,500 Hallmark Gold Crown® stores serve as Hallmark's premiere channel in distributing their products, while another 30,000 retail stores also sell Hallmark products. At any given time, the company offers more than 48,000 various products in thirty languages in more than one hundred countries around the globe.

Every minute of every day, the Hallmark company shares in people's celebrations, through gift wrap, ribbons and bows, napkins, plates and cups, Keepsake Ornaments, books, mugs, and thank you notes. Someplace in the world, Hallmark is there.

Hallmark is committed to remaining a privately-owned company. This is unique. It was the decision of Mr. J. C. Hall, in 1956, that the employees would enjoy profit sharing. This was almost unknown when the program began. The Hallmark company was one of the first to offer coffee breaks to its employees. Through the years, Hallmark has been recognized on the lists of best companies to work for and top companies for working mothers.

Mr. Hall has been quoted as having said this about Hallmark consumers, "Every day people by the millions gain the experience of making decisions about design, color, and words—and, in that sense, they are making meaningful social and aesthetic statements, helping to set national standards of taste." He never lost sight of the fact that the consumer generates what is going to be bought, as well as what products will not sell.

Mr. Hall is quoted as saying, "To ensure that Hallmark cards were in good taste and of the highest quality, each design was reviewed and approved by J. C. Hall and his OK Committee; only those initialed, 'J. C.' went into production."

Mr. J. C. Hall and the OK Committee

Mr. J. C. Hall looking at the new Hallmark headquarters.

Little did that eighteen-year-old young man realize when he stepped off the train in Kansas City that cold, winter day that his two shoe boxes of postcards would grow into the company it is today. Perhaps his greatest asset was an American dream tucked so tightly in his heart that no setback, not even a fire, could destroy his desire to succeed and to give his very best.

Mr. J. C. Hall could easily be called the "Father of Greeting Cards." He took the idea of giving words to people, created a voice for them to be part of special celebrations, gave the most meaningful words to people's losses or joys in their celebrations, and gave laughter through humor. He wanted every design and word to fit the need of any occasion that the human spirit could experience. For people to know that when the Hallmark trademark is seen on any of its products, it was created so that the receiver would know that someone had "cared enough to send or give the very best."

Epilogue

Closing Thoughts

Dear Readers,

My hope is that you have not only learned about the impressive life of Mr. Joyce Clyde Hall and Hallmark Cards, Inc., but that you have gained some knowledge in the area of economics.

The free market/free enterprise system we have in the United States is the key to our many inventions and ideas we enjoy and appreciate today. Entrepreneurs are born when creative minds are free to see and develop new ideas, inventions, and innovations. If a country owns all rights to commerce and trade, the creative minds of its citizens will weaken.

America continues to flourish through the freedom of thought and creativity of its people. Flight, electricity, light bulbs, radios, televisions, Internet, computers, greeting cards, athletic shoes, elevators, cosmetics, clothes, and automobiles were all small parts of American dreams that have come from resourceful people who were free to be their creative selves.

It is my belief that Mr. Joyce Clyde Hall would be pleased to know that in some small way his biography would ignite a light someplace in you as young readers and spark new ideas, so that many of you will become part of the next generation of discoverers, creators, and entrepreneurs.

The persistent making of America depends on all of you giving your very best. We are a country that thrives with the constant revolution of ideas. Mr. Joyce Clyde Hall was one of the many who has contributed to the making of America.

I give you my acknowledgment for completing this biography and study. You will make many economic decisions during your lifetime. Good Luck!

Sincerely,

M. Benedict

Timeline: Major Events in Hallmark's History

1891   Joyce Clyde Hall was born, August 29.

1910   Joyce Hall moved to Kansas City, Missouri to build the postcard business.

1912   Greeting cards were added as postcard interest declined.

1914   Publishing began as the company commissioned twenty engraved Christmas cards.

1915   A fire destroyed the Hall Brothers' office and their entire inventory. The company began publishing its own cards to sell. Postcards read, "Published by Hall Brothers, Kansas City, Missouri, Made in U.S.A."

1916   A retail store was opened in Kansas City.

1917   Gift wrap industry was born as the first product line beyond greeting cards.

1921   Joyce Hall marries Elizabeth Ann Dilday.

1925   "Hallmark" first appeared on products, but "Hall Brothers" appeared on most cards.

1928   Donald Joyce Hall was born. "Hallmark" appears on the backs of all greeting cards. Their first ad appeared in *Ladies' Home Journal*.

1932   Walt Disney characters were used on cards.

1935   The "Eye-Vision" display was patented to help display cards.

1935   Hallmark was one of the first companies to offer employees coffee breaks.

1938   Radio advertising for greeting cards brought the Hallmark name forward.

1939   A Mother's Day card called the "Pansy Card" was introduced and became the number one best-selling card. It is still in Hallmark's line today.

1944   The slogan, "When You Care Enough to Send the Very Best" was first used.

1949   The famous Hallmark signature and crown logo was created.

1950   The Hallmark logo became a registered trademark.

1951   A series of television specials began and became known as the "Hallmark Hall of Fame."

1953   Donald J. Hall joined Hallmark as a salesman.

1954   Hallmark Cards, Inc. became the company's official name.

1956   Company moved into its present location (25th and McGee, Kansas City, Missouri).

1959   Ambassador card line was launched.

1960   Hallmark celebrated its fiftieth anniversary. Partyware and paper products were introduced.

1961   J. C. Hall was the first sponsor awarded an Emmy.

1962 Betsey Clark "Charmers" was introduced.

1966 Donald J. Hall became president and CEO of Hallmark Cards, Inc.

1968 Groundbreaking for Crown Center took place.

1973 Crown Center's first phase was completed. Keepsake Ornaments for Christmas decorating were introduced.

1974 J. C. Hall was honored by the National Association of Greeting Card Publishers.

1975 A permanent "Kaleidoscope" exhibit opened in Crown Center.

1982 Joyce Clyde Hall died at the age of ninety-one on October 29. Presidential Christmas cards were presented to the National Museum of American History—Smithsonian Institution.

1984 Crayola® crayons and art products joined the Hallmark family of companies.

1986 The Shoebox Greetings line was launched.

1986 Irvine O. Hockaday, Jr. was named president and chief executive officer—the first person outside of the Hall family to hold the CEO title. Donald J. Hall continues to serve as chairman of the board.

1987 Hallmark introduced Mahogany cards for African-American consumers.

1995 Tree of Life cards for Jewish consumers were introduced.

1999 Hallmark.com was relaunched and offered free e-cards. In sixty years, 30 million copies of the Pansy greeting card have been sold. "Hallmark en Espanol" cards for Spanish-speaking consumers were introduced. The 52,000 square foot Crown Center Exhibit Hall opened in January.

2001 The Hallmark Channel was launched as a cable television network featuring family-friendly entertainment programming.

2002 Donald J. Hall, Jr., grandson of Hallmark founder, J. C. Hall, was named president and CEO.

2003 Sinceramente Hallmark, an enhanced line of Spanish-language cards, made its premiere.

2004 The Hallmark Channel ranked as a top ten U.S. cable network for the first time.

2005 David E. Hall, grandson of Joyce C. Hall, was promoted to the role of president of Hallmark's personal expression business.

2006 *Hallmark Magazine* debuted—a bimonthly women's lifestyle magazine with a unique storytelling approach.

2007 Hallmark (PRODUCT) RED™ greeting cards were introduced, with a portion of the product sales helping to fight AIDS in Africa. It is the largest social impact initiative in the company's history.

2010 Hallmark will celebrate its centennial years of enriching people's lives.

Glossary Of Terms

Business plan—a document an entrepreneur prepares to describe his or her product, cost, competition, and marketing plan. A formal statement of a company's goals and strategy to achieve them—a road map.

Capital resources—items produced by people and used in the production of goods or resources. Examples include tools, buildings, machines, and computers.

Consumers—those who use goods or services.

Credit—the ability to buy goods and services and pay for them later.

Demand—the amount of goods or services that consumers are willing and able to pay for during some time period, holding other things constant.

Division of labor—occurs when people specialize in one task of a production process.

Economics—the study of how people decide to use their scarce resources to satisfy wants. This includes decisions about production, consumption, and distribution of goods and services.

Entrepreneur—one who risks time, efforts, and funds to bring a product to market.

Goods—things people can buy and use to satisfy wants; we can touch them.

Human resources—people who do mental and/or physical work in our economy.

Interest—the price paid for using someone else's money.

Inventory—goods, supplies, and materials in stock in a company or store.

Logo—a symbol used by a corporation or business as an emblem.

Long-term credit—when you have a longer time to repay money borrowed, usually at a lower interest rate, such as when buying a house.

Natural resources—things that occur naturally upon the earth. Examples include land, water, and minerals.

Opportunity cost—the highest valued alternative given up when a choice is made.

Opportunity recognition—the ability to see the potential of a new idea or product.

Partnership—when two or more people operate a business.

Patent—a document that gives a company or inventor the sole rights to sell or use an invention for a limited period of time.

Product research—knowing what sells and what doesn't sell at a certain price.

Profit—the money remaining after all costs of production are paid. Profit is income for entrepreneurs.

Proprietor(s)—one who owns or shares ownership of a business.

Quantity demanded—the amount of products or services that people are willing and able to buy at a certain price.

Savings—income received that is not spent on consumption; it is set aside.

Scarcity—the condition that occurs when people's wants for goods and services are greater than the resources available.

Services— activities people do for us, like giving haircuts.

Slogan—a short phrase used in a company's advertising.

Substitutes—goods or services that consumers use in place of other goods or services. For example, people buy orange juice in place of apple juice.

Trademark—a manufacturer's or trader's registered emblem or name, used to identify his/her goods.

Venture capital—the money needed to start a business.

Wages—the payment people receive for the work they provide.

Wants—desires that can be satisfied by consuming goods and/or services.

Wholesale—selling something in large quantities that will be sold by a retailer, such as a store.

Selected Bibliography

Joyce C. Hall with Curtiss Anderson, *When You Care Enough.* Kansas City, MO: Hallmark Cards, Inc. 1979, 1992.

Hallmark Corporate Brochure, "Enriching Lives." http://pressroom.hallmark.com/Hmk_corporate_brochure07.pdf

Used with permission. Voluntary National Content Standards in Economics, Copyright 1997, National Council of Economic Education, New York, NY. All rights reserved. For information, visit: www.ncee.net or call 1-800-338-1192.

Web sites:

http://pressroom.hallmark.com
http://stopbullyingnow.hrsa.gov
http://childhelp.org

Innovators' Gallery

Dear Readers,

If you ever become curious about other famous innovators and entrepreneurs, the following is a brief list of some of these great Americans.

Mary Kay Ash—became known as the cosmetics queen.

Frank Ball—patented the Mason jar.

Clarence Birdseye—started Birdseye frozen foods.

Henry Wollman Bloch—founder of H&R Block.

Warren Buffet—outperformed the stock market.

Asa Candler—bought the recipe for Coca-Cola.

James E. Casey—grew company called UPS.

Liz Claiborne—designer of working women's clothing.

Michael Dell—started the mass customization of personal computers.

Charles Drew—invented the blood bank.

Wilbert Gore—invented Gore-Tex.

William Harley and Arthur Davidson—inventors of Harley-Davidson motorcycle.

Howard Head—created high-tech skis and tennis rackets.

Milton Hershey—started the largest candy making company in the world.

Howard Hughes—was an innovative aircraft constructor.

Wayne Huizenga—made Blockbuster Entertainment a videocassette giant.

Herb Kelleher—co-founder of Southwest Airlines.

Ray Kroc—started McDonald's.

George Lucas—changed movies with special effects.

Mary Pickford—co-founder of United Artists.

Howard Schultz—turned a coffee bean shop into Starbucks.

Albert Spalding—built a sporting-goods chain.

Earl S. Tupper—invented Tupperware.

Sam Walton—started Wal-Mart.

Joseph Wilson—developed photocopying technology; Xerox CEO.

Oprah Winfrey—a producer, actress, and television host.

Frank Zambone—invented ice resurfacing machine for skating rinks.

Discussion Questions

Dear Readers,

On the following pages, you will find questions that will hopefully provide further discussions between you and your classmates. There are questions after each chapter. You might bring them to study groups and create conversations that will give you a better understanding of what it means to be an entrepreneur. You will find yourself using the economic terms in this story.

One of the interesting applications that you will find occurs during a study of history. Think about why Columbus came to the Americas. His greatest motivation was that of wanting to be a rich entrepreneur—most intelligent people knew that the world was round. He found that King Ferdinand and Queen Isabella also needed to add more money to their kingdom. They had been fighting a long war and were almost out of money. He had opportunity recognition, but he needed someone to furnish him with venture capital. This is just one of many applications of the vocabulary of economics that you will find in your future studies.

I have added additional pages that will allow you to put your creative muscles to work. There are opportunities to write, create, and problem-solve. Enjoy!

Directions: Please answer the questions with complete sentences.

Chapter 1   Lessons From Poverty

1. What is immediate gratification? Are there times when it is necessary? When?
2. What did you like about the school J. C. attended? Dislike?
3. What are your thoughts about "shared drinking" from the school bucket? Do you "share" with your friends? Is this any different from sharing food or lip gloss?
4. Explain why J. C. didn't complete school. Was it a valid reason?
5. What are the advantages of completing high school today? What economic reasons?
6. What was J. C.'s first job? Would this be possible today?
7. Have you ever had any business experiences? Have you ever earned money? How?

Chapter 2   Growing and Learning

1. Do you have a savings account at a bank or at home? Is it difficult to save? What are some of the ways you and your family can save money? How did saving money effect Mr. Hall's life when a business opportunity came his way? Hint: Remember the popcorn?
2. Why was J. C. not in the habit of spending? Discuss with a partner in your classroom why you are part of the family budget when you spend money. Name the items that are bought just for you—for the family.
3. What activities might keep you from working the long hours that J. C. worked?
4. How many of the books mentioned in this chapter have you read?
5. What evidence suggests that J. C. was used as a scapegoat?
6. Why did J. C. take a gun when he traveled with Rollie? Are things different today?
7. What crucial decision did J. C. make the summer he took Rollie's candy route?
8. Perhaps you have a family story that you enjoy telling. Is it funny, sad, or exciting? Write some brief details, and share it with a partner.

Chapter 3   Going to Kansas City

1. The text infers that people valued their postcards. What makes any collection have value?

2. J. C. had to convince his brothers that the postcard business was a good idea. Have you ever had to convince anyone that you had a good idea? When?

3. Explain a time when you used "opportunity recognition" to convince your parents of something you wanted to do or buy.

4. What part of looking at a "profit" did the Hall brothers leave out?

5. For what three reasons was Kansas City a place of opportunity?

6. J. C.'s first home and office measured 12 × 12 feet. Measure your classroom and compare.

7. J. C. created a business plan. Describe something that you have done that required a plan. (Hint: Travel plans with family; time management)

8. J. C. considered being absent from his family as his greatest opportunity cost. List five choices/opportunity costs you have made. Share with a partner. Be ready to share one with the class.

Chapter 4   Building an Unknown Future

1. Name one part of J. C. and Rollie's sales philosophy.

2. How does quantity demand (the amount of a product or service that people are willing and able to buy) affect a business? Can you think of products that are no longer in demand?

3. J. C. identified with the words on the postcard saying, "When you get to the end of your rope, tie on a knot, and hang on." What factors caused him to identify with these words?

4. Name some inventory that you would find in a grocery store.

5. What is scarcity? How has the situation of scarcity affected your life?

Chapter 5   Economic Changes and New Growth

1. Why did Mr. Hall think that greeting cards would continue to be bought during the economic depression?

2. Why are famous people used in advertising? Name some.

3. Why are products patented? Why do you think the Eye-Vision fixture helped the business dealers?

4. Hallmark's slogan is, "When you care enough to send the very best." What slogans do you know that are used today in advertisements?

5. Write a slogan for your school, family, friends, or town.

Chapter 6   Mr. Hall and His Family

1. "The family wanted to name his son Joyce, but Mr. Hall didn't want his child having a girl's name." What does this quote infer? Do you know any names that either a girl or a boy could have? Is the spelling usually different?
2. How did Del Masco help Rollie and Mr. Hall? Tell a "heroic" dog story.
3. Name three steps that led to Mr. Donald Hall, Sr. becoming President of Hallmark Cards, Inc. Why were these steps important?
4. What were Mr. Hall's most cherished assets?
5. Draw your family tree.

Chapter 7   Progress of New Ideas

1. What did you learn about President Eisenhower?
2. What was unique about the first Emmy given to Mr. Hall?
3. Explain the statement, "He (Mr. J. C. Hall) didn't have in mind what would later become the bridge between his company and downtown Kansas City."
4. Visualizing Crown Center, what do you see?
5. Name the *human resources* of one of the following: grocery store, doctor's office, school, auto factory, hospital, fast food restaurant, home improvement store, or bookstore.
6. Name the *capital resources* of the business you chose.
7. What did Mr. Hall consider were the two main components of a greeting card?
8. Why would you want to work for a privately-owned company that offers profit sharing?

Creative Work For Students

Name _____

Goods and Services. Please make a list for the following:

Goods: things people buy and use to satisfy wants; we can touch them.
Services: activities people do for us.

Goods	Services

Making Inferences

Quote	Inference
"J.C. sometimes observed that when food was scarce, his mother didn't seem very hungry."	
"Even at that time cigarettes were referred to as 'coffin nails.'"	
"Masco died the next day on the vet's examining table."	
"Crown Center has been compared to an ancient marketplace like the Forum in Rome, Italy."	
"He wanted every design and word to fit the need of any occasion that the human spirit could experience."	
"If a country owns all rights to commerce and trade, the creative minds of its citizens will weaken."	

Name _____

When J.C. Hall was eleven years old, working at his brother's bookstore, he earned $18.00 a month—$4.50 a week. The first prices of goods below were taken from a 1903 catalogue. The second prices are comparable to today's prices. Using your calculator, what was the percentage of increase? Hint: Divide the 1903 price by the current price.

Item	1903 Price	Current Price	Percent of Increase
Men's overcoat	$10.00	$229.00	
Men's leather shoes	2.55	75.00	
Men's shirt	.85	40.00	
Men's socks	.27	5.00	
Bicycle	15.75	249.00	
Hammer	.47	16.00	
Bedroom suite	13.95	997.00	
Ladies skirt	1.35	44.00	
Women's hosiery	.20	5.50	
Leather purse	.95	58.00	
Doll	.50	39.99	
Bed comforter	.47	24.99	
Baby carriage (stroller)	8.50	215.00	

Name _____

"During the 1970s, Mr. Hall stated that research showed that people preferred verse to prose in their greeting cards." Over time, that preference has shifted, with more people today choosing shorter, conversational prose over longer verse. Which do you like better? Compose two messages for the inside of a greeting card—one in verse and one in prose.

EXAMPLE: Verse

Twinkle, twinkle little star.

What an amazing child you are.

In my heart you will always live.

I hold dear the joy you give.

EXAMPLE: Prose

You are a shining star, my child

With the wonderful things you do.

You will always live in my heart.

And continue to give me joy.

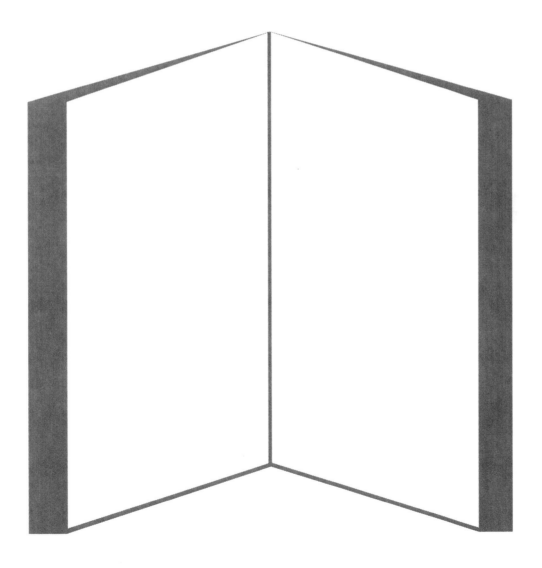

Creative Ideas!

The Topic Is Scarcity

Scarcity is the condition that occurs when people's wants for goods and services are greater than the resources available. (Example: Remember when the Hall brothers ran out of wrapping paper?)

Work with a partner to prepare a fable (a story written to teach a lesson) about scarcity.

Dramatize your fable for a classroom presentation.

Create a collage depicting Mr. Hall's Life

Be creative—your collage should be colorful and informative.

List the milestones of his life. These milestones will then become part of your collage.

Mock Interview

Prepare a mock interview with Mr. Hall to be used on television.

Demonstrate your knowledge of Mr. Hall's life by creating open-ended questions—avoid one-word answers. An example: How did poverty affect your life?

To the Classroom Teacher

With the crowded curriculum that classroom teachers face today, the purpose of this book is to combine social studies and economics vocabulary with reading/literature. This book could be taught either through team teaching or by a single classroom teacher, depending on the structure of your school.

Teachers and students have always enjoyed sharing a story. This biography is about one of America's entrepreneurs, Mr. Joyce Clyde Hall, founder of Hallmark Cards, Inc., and lends itself to learning the vocabulary of economics. All fifty states have adopted NCEE's Voluntary National Content Standards in Economics. Many state exams have excluded social studies, but it remains a part of the curriculum of school districts.

I was a classroom teacher for thirty-four years, and sometimes when given one more thing to teach, my next question would be, "You want me to teach what, when?" That's why this book was written in the format it is. My desire is that as a classroom teacher, you will find this an interesting way to continue the study of economics vocabulary, combined with reading/literature/English.

I highly recommend that this book be read at the beginning of the school year, but it is not necessary. Wars, elections, depressions, inflations, and trade are woven within the threads of economics. During the school year, this study will give you and your students the opportunity to refer to the vocabulary of economics—a constant review!

The pages for the students that are included in this guide are based on the idea of multiple-intelligence and reading/language strategies that work. You may find that some of the pages simply don't fill some needs of your students. None were intended to be "busy work," but to meet each student's unique way of learning. Hopefully, there will be some project or activity that will accomplish that goal. It is not necessary to copy all of the pages! Assignments can be written on the board.

Listen to what students say, and pay attention to what they write! They really don't see themselves as part of the family budget when they want to buy something; they have little understanding that credit card use is borrowing or that we live in a free market/free enterprise economy. They have little experience at saving!

I have found that economics is an interesting and sometimes bewildering study. Yet it is vital that our students are given some idea of economics, and how it reflects our thinking. It affects all of us our entire lives. Most classroom teachers are not economists; we leave that to other professionals, and yet we must meet the expected standards.

Standards addressed were: 1, 2, 3, 6, 7, 8, 9, 10, 13, 14, and 19. (See permission from NCEE. Use their web site.)

Your Federal Reserve Bank is a major source of information and seminars. Please feel free to contact me at maggiegoes@aol.com

Introducing The Book:
Suggestions For The Classroom Teacher

You will need:

Transparency of Prologue

    Four sheets of chart paper for:

        Innovative ideas from products at home

        Changes in parent's lifetime

        Changes in student's lifetime

        List of entrepreneurs and qualities that identify them.

Copy of task and grading schedule for each student.

Copy of grading schedule for final grade for teacher's use.

Day 1: Introducing the Prologue:

1. Teacher reads text orally using transparency of Prologue.

2. As teacher reads, students will volunteer important words/phrases while teacher highlights words/phrases. Discussion follows: Review third person narrative style with class.

3. Possible whole class questions for discussion:

   a. Different ways of using money
   b. What does it mean to risk time, effort, and funds?
   c. "All business is a risk."
   d. What are some innovations in new products?

4. Homework:

   a. How have things changed in your parent's lifetime/your lifetime?
   b. With parents' help, what is an entrepreneur?
   c. List five entrepreneurs and qualities that describe them.
   d. What products in your home offer innovative ideas? Examples: Fat-free foods, high-definition TV.

DAY 2: To the teacher: HOMEWORK DISCUSSIONS:

1. With a partner, agree on one innovative idea from products in your home, one thing that has changed in your lifetime, as well as those of your parents. Students will have a list of three ideas to share with the class.

2. **Topic headings for chart paper:**

   a. Innovative ideas from products at home
   b. Changes in a parent's lifetime
   c. Changes in your lifetime
   d. List of entrepreneurs and qualities that identify them.
   e. Brainstorm a list of entrepreneurs and qualities that identify them.

3. Task (Give students a task and grading schedule sheet.)

   a. Students will research an entrepreneur of their choice:
   b. Information will be presented on 10 × 18 paper or poster board.
   c. Paper or poster must include accomplishments of this entrepreneur with support from his/her life. (Focus on qualities of entrepreneur on chart paper.)

Presentation Ideas (can include combination of ideas for final product)

1. poem
2. timeline
3. diary entry
4. brochure
5. picture book
6. large postcard, no bigger than 8 × 10 paper
7. prose, short stories from his/her life
8. graph
9. graphic organizers
10. visuals from magazines, Internet
11. collage
12. relevant words and phrases
13. other ideas?

Name _____

Present the grading schedule to students as they read their copy.

ENTREPRENEUR POSTER

CREATIVITY	(how it's different)	__/20
CONTENT	(what it says)	__/50
NEATNESS	(how it looks)	__/20
SPELLING/GRAMMAR	(editing)	__/10
	TOTAL	__/100

COMMENTS:

To the student:

Name   _____

Due Date   _____

Task   _____

You will research an entrepreneur of your choice.

1. Information will be presented on 10 × 18 paper or poster board.
2. Paper or poster must include accomplishments of this entrepreneur with support from the person's life. (Focus on qualities of entrepreneur on chart paper.)

PRESENTATION IDEAS (can include combination of ideas for final product):

1. timeline
2. diary entry
3. brochure
4. picture book
5. large postcard, no bigger than 8 × 10 paper
6. prose, short stories from his/her life
7. graph
8. graphic organizers
9. visuals from magazines, Internet
10. collage
11. relevant words and phrases
12. poem
13. other ideas?

For the student:

Grading Schedule

ENTREPRENEUR POSTER EVALUATION:

Name _____

Grading Schedule

ENTREPRENEUR POSTER

CREATIVITY	(how it's different)	__/20
CONTENT	(what it says)	__/50
NEATNESS	(how it looks)	__/20
SPELLING/GRAMMAR	(editing)	__/10
	TOTAL	__/100

Standards and Benchmarks

Standards in the book: *Mr. Joyce Clyde Hall, Founder of Hallmark Cards, Inc.*:

Standard 1: Productive resources are limited. Therefore, people cannot have all the goods and services they want; as a result, they must choose some things and give up others.

Benchmarks: 1, 2, 3, 4, 5, 6, 7, 8, 9, 10, 11, 12, 13, 14, 15.

Standard 2: Effective decision making requires comparing the additional costs of alternatives with the additional benefits. Most choices involve doing a little more or a little less of something; few choices are "all or nothing" decisions.

Benchmarks: 1, 2.

Standard 6: When individuals, regions, and nations specialize in what they can produce at the lowest cost and then trade with others, both production and consumption increases.

Benchmarks: 1, 2, 3.

Standard 7: Markets exist when buyers and sellers interact. This interaction determines market prices and thereby allocates scarce goods and services.

Benchmarks: 1, 2, 3.

Standard 9: Competition among sellers lowers cost and prices and encourages companies to produce more of what consumers are willing and able to buy. Competition among buyers increases prices and allocates goods and services to those people who are willing and able to pay the most for them.

Benchmarks: 1, 2.

Standard 10: Institutions evolve in market economies to help individuals and groups accomplish their goals. Banks, labor unions, corporations, legal systems, and not-for-profit organizations are examples of important institutions. A different kind of institution, clearly defined and enforced property rights, is essential to a market economy.

Benchmarks: 1, 2.

Standard 11: Money makes it easier to trade, borrow, save, invest, and compare the value of goods and services.

Benchmarks: 3, 4.

Standard 13: Income for most people is determined by the market value of the productive resources they sell. What workers earn depends primarily on the market value for what they produce and how productive they are.

Benchmarks: 1, 2.

Standard 14: Entrepreneurs are people who take the risks of organizing productive resources to make goods and services. Profit is an important incentive that leads entrepreneurs to accept the risks of business failure.

Benchmarks: 1, 2, 3.

CPSIA information can be obtained at www.ICGtesting.com
Printed in the USA
BVOW051218020112

279568BV00001B/1/P